# The Mystery
# Mask

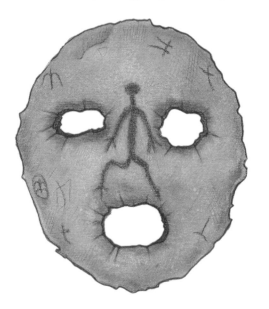

David Calcutt
Illustrated by Robert Eberz

A Harcourt Achieve Imprint

www.Rigby.com
1-800-531-5015

Literacy by Design Leveled Readers: *The Mystery Mask*

ISBN-13:  978-1-4189-3671-6
ISBN-10:      1-4189-3671-5

Printed in China
3 4 5 6 7 8  985  14 13 12 11 10 09 08

# Contents

# **Chapter 1**
## A Trip to the Desert

Uncle Dan pulled the van off the road and switched off the engine. He turned around and said to Annie and Will, "Well, here we are."

Annie and Will were puzzled because Aunt Maggie and Uncle Dan had said they were going on a trip to the desert, but this wasn't the desert! It was just the top of a very long and very steep hill.

They'd been driving up the hill for nearly two hours, with a stop for drinks and a snack about an hour ago. They felt sure they should have reached the desert by now.

"Thought you might want to stretch your legs," said Uncle Dan.

"Good idea!" agreed Aunt Maggie, who was sitting in the front seat next to Uncle Dan. "That mountain road just seems to get longer and longer."

A thumping noise came from the rear seat behind Annie and Will. It sounded like somebody had a drum back there and was beating it hard with both hands.

It was just Bella's tail. Bella was Aunt Maggie and Uncle Dan's brown-and-white springer spaniel. Whenever the dog was excited, she wagged her tail, and she wagged her tail most of the time.

"We'll let Bella out for a stretch, too," said Uncle Dan. "You want to bring her, Annie?"

"Yes, please," Annie said. She and Bella had already become good friends, although Will was still a little bit nervous around her. So when Aunt Maggie opened the rear door, clipped the leash to the dog's collar, and handed the other end to Annie, Will made sure he stood a few paces back.

"It's OK," reassured Annie, "she won't hurt you."

Bella was jumping and wiggling excitedly around Annie's legs.

"That's right," said Aunt Maggie with a laugh. "She might bounce, but she never bites!"

Uncle Dan had already walked on ahead, down a gravel path toward a small picnic space, where there was a table and bench and a painted wooden sign that said "Overlook."

Just beyond the sign, there was a row
of bushes and a metal fence, and beyond
that was the sky, like a huge, bright
blue canopy.

Aunt Maggie called out to him, "Is it still there, Dan?"

"It's still there!" Uncle Dan called back, laughing.

Aunt Maggie smiled at Annie and Will. "Let's go take a look," she said, and she walked down the path toward Uncle Dan.

Annie and Will exchanged looks that said, "What's going on?" It seemed as if Uncle Dan and Aunt Maggie were sharing some kind of secret joke between them, but Annie and Will couldn't be sure.

Uncle Dan was their mother's older brother, and they didn't get to see him and Aunt Maggie too often. Annie and Will had flown out with their parents to visit their aunt and uncle about thirty miles outside of San Diego, in Southern California.

They liked Uncle Dan with his big beard and twinkling eyes and Aunt Maggie with her flowery dresses and jingling bracelets. But what could they want them to see that was so special here at the roadside?

Annie and Will walked down the path to where Uncle Dan was standing, Bella leading the way, pulling at the leash. Uncle Dan told Bella to sit, and she did, though her tail was still wagging in the dust.

"Now," said Aunt Maggie, "just take a look out there."

They looked. They were about a mile up, and below them was a steep drop. Beyond that was the desert.

There it lay, like a great, still, golden ocean, stretching out before them into the distance. Annie and Will stared, and for a moment or two they didn't speak, but when they did, they both said together, "Wow!"

# **Chapter 2**
## It's Hot out There!

Annie and Will lived on the East Coast. They had never been in an airplane before, they had never driven up into the mountains before, and they had never seen the desert before.

But now they were actually in the desert!

While their mother and father were sightseeing in San Diego, Uncle Dan and Aunt Maggie had told Annie and Will they would be going on a mystery trip, and this was it.

Having come down out of the mountains, the group was now driving along a straight road that led right across the desert as far as the eye could see. Aunt Maggie said that it went on like this for more than 300 miles before it reached the next town.

Will was wondering if that was where they were going, and if they could get there and back in time for supper, when suddenly Uncle Dan turned off the road onto a track that led to the right.

The track was heading directly toward a high cliff of red rocks. Uncle Dan pulled up to the foot of the cliff and switched off the van's engine.

"Hats on heads, boots on feet," said Aunt Maggie, smiling, "and bring a bottle of water each. It's hot out there."

It *was* hot. When they'd gotten out of the van at the top of the mountain, there'd been a sharp chill in the air, but down here the sun was fierce and the light was clear and bright. Annie looked into the distance where the desert glittered as if it were filled with diamonds. Strange plants that looked like green, spiky fingers stuck up out of the ground. Everywhere the air trembled in the heat; it looked as if the sky itself were melting.

Annie took a drink from her bottle of water, and then they set off along a narrow path that led upward among the rocks. Bella led the way, pulling on her leash as she ran up along the track, stopping and waiting for them to catch up, then heading off again, dragging Aunt Maggie along behind her. Annie and Will walked behind Aunt Maggie and Uncle Dan.

"Where do you think we're going?" asked Will.

Annie shrugged. Maybe they weren't going anywhere, just walking in the desert. She didn't mind–she liked the desert–but there was one thing that was puzzling her.

When they had left the van, Uncle Dan had taken a large flashlight with him. Why would they need a flashlight?

"It's like going on a mystery adventure, isn't it?" she said to Will.

The track became level and turned off to the left. They stopped. In front of them there was a hollow in the rock, high and wide—a cave! They stood at the entrance and peered in. It was dark and cool in there, and when Bella barked, her voice echoed inside.

"Take a look in here," Aunt Maggie said to Annie and Will, and she had that smile and shiny light in her eyes again.

Now Annie found out what the flashlight was for. As they stepped into the cave, Uncle Dan turned on the flashlight and held it up. They saw that the walls of the cave were covered with pictures of animals, birds, and people.

There were strange-looking creatures and stick figures with long, wavy arms and legs. It was like stepping into another world. The flashlight made shadows on the walls, so that the pictures seemed to be alive and moving. The whole cave was full of a strange kind of life.

"Well," said Uncle Dan, "what do you think?"

Annie and Will stared, and for a moment or two, they didn't speak, but when they did, they both said together, "Wow!"

# **Chapter 3**
## A Doggone Discovery

The group stayed in the cave for a while and then started back down the track. This time, instead of pulling on the leash, Bella explored all around her, sniffing everything she could find. Sometimes all the others could see of her was her tail wagging from behind a rock. As they walked, Aunt Maggie and Uncle Dan told Will and Annie about the people who had painted the pictures in the cave.

The people were called the Kumeyaay, and they once lived all over Southern California. There were several caves filled with their pictures, some of them painted onto the rock, some of them scratched into it. The oldest pictures were made thousands of years ago. The pictures told stories of the Kumeyaay—their history, their religion, their way of life. The cave was like a book—a huge stone book.

Uncle Dan told Will one of the stories, about a character called Coyote who was always playing tricks and getting into trouble.

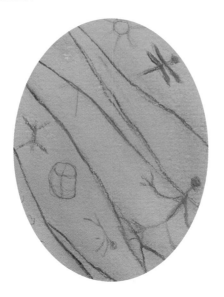

Annie asked Aunt Maggie if other people knew about the paintings, and Aunt Maggie told her that the cave was looked after by a museum in San Diego. If you wanted to visit the cave, you had to ask the museum first, which Uncle Dan had done a few days before.

Suddenly Annie turned around and asked, "Where is Bella?"

Everyone stopped and looked, but Bella was nowhere to be seen—not even her tail wagging from behind a rock. Uncle Dan called her, but she didn't appear. Aunt Maggie put her fingers in her mouth and gave a loud whistle, but still there was no sign of the dog. Aunt Maggie and Uncle Dan looked worried. "I can't believe I let go of her leash," Aunt Maggie said.

"I hope she's all right," said Will.

"Listen," said Uncle Dan, "I can hear her!"

Bella was barking, but her bark was faint, as if it were coming from inside the rocks.

Suddenly Will pointed to a pile of large rocks a few yards away and cried out, "Look! There she is!"

Poking out from between the rocks was the tip of a brown-and-white wagging tail. They hurried over to the rocks, where they could see the tail coming from a large hole.

"Hey, Bella," called Uncle Dan, "come on out of there!"

Bella gave another muffled bark and her tail vanished into the hole.

They heard a scuffling noise, then Bella's head appeared and she came scrambling out of the hole with something dark and leathery in her mouth. She dropped it and wagged her tail even harder.

"It's some kind of old animal hide," said Aunt Maggie, picking it up and looking at it. It was stiff and hard and oval shaped. The surface was covered in little scratch marks, and there were three holes in it, two near the top, and a larger one near the bottom.

"It looks like a face," Will said.

Then they all realized what it was—a mask!

"It's a very old mask," said Uncle Dan. "It must have been down in that hole for a long time."

"But where did it come from, and who'd want to put a mask down a hole?" asked Annie.

"It's a real mystery," said Aunt Maggie.

Will had been looking at the scratch marks on the mask, and suddenly he shouted, "They're like the pictures in the cave!"

Will was right. The scratch marks were like some of the figures in the cave. Annie remembered the one with long, wavy arms and legs, and it was right there on the mask.

"Do you think it's a Kumeyaay mask?" asked Annie.

"It could be," said Uncle Dan, "but there's only one way to find out, and that's to take it to the museum."

# Chapter 4
## At the Museum

Later that afternoon, the group arrived at the museum in San Diego. Annie and Will's mom and dad were waiting there because Uncle Dan had called to say what they were doing. They all went inside the museum except for Aunt Maggie, who stayed outside with Bella.

A woman was waiting to greet them. She told them her name was Maria and that she was one of the curators.

"What's a curator?" asked Will.

"Someone who looks after the museum," said Mom.

"That's right," said Maria, "and I look after the artifacts from the Kumeyaay people."

Will looked puzzled again and asked, "What's an artifact?"

"It's just a fancy word for an old object," Maria replied, smiling, "and this old object you found is very interesting. May I see it?"

Annie handed the mask to Maria, and while Maria was looking at it, Will told her that they thought the scratch marks looked like the pictures in the cave.

Annie showed her the stick figure with the wavy arms and legs. It was drawn right down the middle of the mask, in between the holes for the eyes and the mouth.

"You're both very sharp," Maria said. "These *are* Kumeyaay figures, and that figure in the middle is one of the most important. That's Coyote. In fact, this might be a mask of Coyote himself."

Will's eyes opened wide, and his mouth did too, but he didn't say anything.

Maria then told them she would try to find out as much about the mask as she could. After that it would go into a display case in the museum with a card next to it saying what it was, where it was found, and who found it.

Annie and Will were thrilled that their names were going to be in a display case. Everyone who came to the museum would see them, but they wanted Bella's name to go on display as well.

"Bella's our dog," Uncle Dan explained to Maria, "and she was the one who found the mask."

So Maria agreed that Bella's name would definitely have to go on the card, too.

As they were leaving the museum, Will said, "Uncle Dan was telling me a story about Coyote, and that's when we found the mask."

Uncle Dan looked thoughtful, and this made Annie ask, "Do you think that's strange, Uncle Dan?"

"I'll tell you what I think it is," he said. "I think it's another mystery!"

# Chapter 5
## The Mystery of the Mask

About a week later, Aunt Maggie called Annie and Will in from the yard where they were playing with Bella. She said that they all had to go back to the museum because the curator had phoned about the mask.

When Maria met them again at the museum, there was a man with her whom they had not seen before.

He had gray hair, wore glasses, and was dressed in a suit, so he looked important. Maria introduced him as Mr. Carlos Sanchez, an elder of the Kumeyaay people. She'd told him about the mask, and he'd wanted to meet the people who had found it.

Mr. Sanchez smiled down at Annie and Will and said, "The mask is very special to our people. It's very old—although no one is really sure how old it is—and for a long time it has been lost." He told them how the mask had mysteriously vanished more than two hundred years before.

Mr. Sanchez also said that no one knew how or why the mask vanished, or who might have taken it—but the Kumeyaay always hoped that one day they would find it again.

"And now it has been found," said Mr. Sanchez, "thanks to you two!"

"And to Bella," said Will.

Mr. Sanchez gave Annie and Will little plaques with their names on them. On each plaque was a picture of the mask with the figure with wavy arms and legs, and underneath were the words, "A true friend of the Kumeyaay people."

Then they had their picture taken with Mr. Sanchez. It was in the paper the next week: there was Mr. Sanchez in the middle, with Annie on the right and Will on the left, both holding their plaques. And, of course, sitting in front of Mr. Sanchez, with her fur freshly brushed, was Bella!

A week after that, Will and Annie flew home. During the flight, Will suddenly turned to Annie and said, "I wonder how the mask got down into that hole in the rocks."

"It's another mystery," said Annie, "and I don't suppose we'll ever know the answer to it."

"No," said Will, "but we can have fun trying to figure it out."

And that's just what they did for the rest of the flight.